RUSSIAN TORTOISE

Russian Tortoise Care Guide: Comprehensive Advice On Habitat, Nutrition, Health, Behavior, Interaction, Socialization, Hatchling, Feeding, Lighting, Handling, Mating, And Breeding

Ethan Harry

Table of Contents

CHAPTER ONE

INTRODUCTION TO RUSSIAN TORTOISES

Overview Of Russian Tortoises

Russian tortoises, known scientifically as Testudo horsfieldii, are small, robust reptiles native to the arid regions of Central Asia, encompassing countries such as Russia, Uzbekistan, Kazakhstan, and Afghanistan. They have become popular pets due to their manageable size, distinctive personalities, and relatively straightforward care requirements.

One of the most striking features of Russian tortoises is their domed shells, which offer protection and contribute to their hardy nature. These shells come in various shades of brown and olive, often with distinct dark markings that add to their visual appeal. Their sturdy limbs are well-adapted to their native, often rugged terrain, enabling them to dig and navigate through challenging environments effectively.

Russian tortoises are relatively small compared to many other tortoise species, which makes them particularly appealing to reptile enthusiasts who may lack the space required for larger tortoises. Typically, adult Russian tortoises reach a length of 5-10 inches, with males generally being smaller than females. Their compact size, combined with their resilience, makes them an ideal choice for those new to tortoise care or for experienced keepers looking to add a smaller species to their collection.

In their natural habitat, Russian tortoises are found in dry, grassy areas and deserts, where they have adapted to the extreme conditions. These environments require them to be resourceful and resilient, traits that they bring into captivity. In the wild, they are known to dig extensive burrows to escape the heat and find moisture, a behavior that can also be observed in captivity if they are provided with appropriate substrate.

Caring for Russian tortoises involves creating an environment that mimics their natural habitat as closely as possible. This includes providing a spacious enclosure with a dry substrate suitable for burrowing, such as a mix of soil and sand. A basking area with a heat source is essential, as these tortoises require temperatures between 90-100°F during the day to thrive. Additionally, UVB lighting is crucial for their health, helping them to metabolize calcium and maintain strong shells and bones.

Diet-wise, Russian tortoises are herbivores and primarily consume a variety of leafy greens, vegetables, and some fruits. A diet rich in fiber and low in protein is necessary to prevent health issues and mimic their natural foraging behaviors. Fresh water should always be available, and regular soaking can help keep them hydrated.

With their engaging personalities, Russian tortoises can become quite interactive with their owners, recognizing them and even showing curiosity. Their long lifespan, often exceeding 40 years in captivity with proper care, means they can be lifelong companions, offering many years of enjoyment and learning for their keepers.

Natural Habitat And Distribution

Russian tortoises (Agrionemys horsfieldii) are native to arid environments characterized by extreme seasonal variations. Their natural habitats include dry, scrubby areas, deserts, and rocky hillsides. These regions are subject to dramatic temperature fluctuations, with scorching hot summers and freezing cold winters. To survive these harsh climates, Russian tortoises have evolved into proficient burrowers. They dig extensive and deep tunnels, which provide refuge from the extreme temperatures and potential predators. These burrows create a stable microenvironment, offering consistent conditions that are crucial for their survival.

In the wild, Russian tortoises can be found across a broad swath of Central Asia. Their distribution spans several countries, including Russia, Kazakhstan, Uzbekistan, Turkmenistan, and parts of Iran, Afghanistan, and Pakistan. This wide geographic range showcases their remarkable adaptability, as they can thrive in diverse environmental conditions. The ability to inhabit such varied landscapes is a testament to their resilience and evolutionary success.

However, the natural populations of Russian tortoises face significant threats. Habitat destruction is a major concern, as human activities such as agriculture, urban development, and mining encroach upon their natural habitats. The alteration and fragmentation of their environments reduce the available space and resources necessary for their survival. Additionally, over-collection for the pet trade poses a severe risk to their wild populations. Russian tortoises are popular in the pet industry due to their manageable size and relatively easy care requirements, leading to extensive capture and exportation from their native habitats. This exploitation has significantly diminished their numbers in the wild.

The decline in Russian tortoise populations underscores the importance of conservation efforts. Protecting their natural habitats is crucial for their continued survival. Conservation strategies may include establishing protected areas, restoring degraded habitats, and implementing regulations to control the collection and trade of these tortoises. Public awareness campaigns can also play a vital role in reducing the demand for wild-caught tortoises and promoting responsible pet ownership.

Physical Characteristics

Russian tortoises exhibit a range of distinctive physical characteristics that make them easily identifiable among other tortoise species. Their shells are particularly notable; they are rounded and domed with a relatively flattened top. The coloration of their shells is generally brown or olive, interspersed with darker patches. This natural coloration provides excellent camouflage, helping them blend seamlessly into their arid, rocky habitats, thereby offering protection from predators.

The shells of Russian tortoises serve multiple functions beyond mere protection. They are integral to the tortoises' ability to survive in harsh environments, as they store both fat and water. This capability is crucial for enduring the arid conditions of their native habitats, where water can be scarce. These adaptations enable the tortoises to thrive in regions with limited resources, showcasing their remarkable evolutionary resilience.

Size is another distinctive feature of Russian tortoises. Adult individuals typically range from 5 to 10 inches in length. Females are generally larger than males, a trait that is linked to their reproductive roles. The larger body size of females allows them to carry more eggs, thereby increasing their reproductive success. This sexual dimorphism is a common adaptation in many animal species, where the physical differences between genders are often related to their specific reproductive strategies.

The limbs of Russian tortoises are robust and well-adapted for their lifestyle. Their legs are strong and covered in scales, equipped with sharp claws designed for digging. This adaptation is essential for their burrowing behavior, which is a key aspect of their survival strategy. Burrows provide shelter from extreme temperatures and predators, making them a vital component of the tortoises' daily lives. Unlike many other tortoise species, Russian tortoises possess only four toes on each front foot, rather than the more typical five. This unique trait further distinguishes them from their relatives and is a useful identifying feature.

The heads of Russian tortoises are proportionally small, yet they are perfectly suited to their dietary needs. They have dark, expressive eyes and a beak-like mouth. This specialized mouth structure is ideal for their herbivorous diet, allowing them to efficiently graze on a variety of vegetation. Their diet typically includes grasses, leafy plants, and flowers, which they forage for in their natural habitats.

Lifespan And Growth

Russian tortoises are known for their impressive lifespan, especially when compared to many other small pets. In captivity, they can live for 40 to 50 years or even longer with the right care and environment. Their longevity makes them a long-term commitment for any potential owner. In contrast, their lifespan in the wild is typically shorter due to various factors such as predation, habitat loss, and environmental challenges. These challenges can significantly impact their survival, highlighting the importance of conservation efforts in their natural habitats.

The growth rate of Russian tortoises is influenced by several factors, including diet, environment, and genetics. At hatching, they are about the size of a ping pong ball and measure just a few inches in length. As they grow, their shells develop the characteristic domed shape, and their coloration darkens and becomes more distinct. This growth is most rapid during the first few years of life, but it slows considerably as they approach maturity.

A proper diet is crucial for the healthy growth of Russian tortoises. In captivity, they thrive on a diet rich in leafy greens, such as dandelion greens, collard greens, and mustard greens, along with a variety of vegetables. While fruits can be offered occasionally, they should not constitute a significant portion of their diet due to the high sugar content. It's essential to provide a balanced diet to ensure they receive the necessary nutrients for growth and health.

Creating an appropriate habitat is equally important for the well-being and growth of Russian tortoises. They require an environment that closely mimics their natural habitat, which includes access to adequate heat, lighting, and a suitable substrate for digging. Temperature regulation is vital, with a basking area that reaches about 90-95°F and a cooler area that allows for temperature variation. Providing access to UVB light is essential, as it helps the tortoises synthesize vitamin D3, which is crucial for calcium absorption and healthy shell development. Without proper UVB exposure, tortoises can develop metabolic bone disease, leading to serious health issues.

CHAPTER TWO

ACQUIRING A RUSSIAN TORTOISE

Choosing A Healthy Tortoise

Choosing a healthy Russian tortoise is essential for ensuring a long and happy life for your new pet. Here's a detailed guide on what to look for to make the best choice:

1. Active and Alert: The first sign of a healthy tortoise is its level of activity and alertness. A healthy Russian tortoise should move around confidently and respond to its surroundings. Its eyes should be bright and clear, indicating good health and vitality. An inactive or lethargic tortoise might be sick or stressed, which can lead to further health issues down the line.

2. Shell Condition: Examine the tortoise's shell meticulously. A healthy tortoise's shell should be smooth, hard, and free of cracks or unusual bumps. A soft or deformed shell can be a sign of malnutrition, poor living conditions, or metabolic bone disease, which is common in tortoises that haven't received adequate care. Look for a well-formed shell with even growth patterns, as irregularities can indicate underlying health problems.

3. Skin and Limbs: The skin and limbs of a Russian tortoise are other critical indicators of health. The skin should be clean and free of sores, cuts, or signs of infection. The limbs should be strong and able to retract fully into the shell

when the tortoise feels threatened. Weakness in the limbs or inability to retract could suggest health issues, including metabolic bone disease or injury.

4. Eating Habits: Observing the tortoise's eating habits can provide significant insight into its health. A healthy Russian tortoise will have a good appetite and show interest in food. If possible, watch the tortoise during feeding time. A lack of interest in food or difficulty eating can be signs of illness or stress. Ensure that the tortoise is fed a proper diet of leafy greens and vegetables, which is crucial for their health and well-being.

5. Breathing: Listen carefully to the tortoise's breathing. It should be quiet and steady. Wheezing, clicking sounds, or labored breathing can indicate respiratory issues, which are common in tortoises exposed to poor living conditions or drastic changes in temperature and humidity. Respiratory infections can be severe and require veterinary attention, so it's important to ensure the tortoise is breathing normally before making a purchase.

6. Behavior: Finally, observe the tortoise's behavior. A healthy Russian tortoise should exhibit normal behavior for its species. This means they should be curious and responsive to their environment. Watch how it interacts

with its surroundings, other tortoises, and humans. A tortoise that hides constantly, appears overly shy, or behaves erratically might be under stress or suffering from health issues.

Legal And Ethical Considerations

Acquiring a tortoise involves significant legal and ethical responsibilities that potential owners must take seriously. Firstly, it is crucial to familiarize yourself with the local laws and regulations regarding the ownership of Russian tortoises. Different regions may have specific requirements or may mandate permits for keeping these reptiles as pets. Non-compliance with these laws can lead to legal issues, fines, and the possible confiscation of your pet.

When sourcing your tortoise, it is essential to purchase from reputable breeders or rescue organizations. These sources are more likely to ensure that the animals are kept in humane conditions and receive proper care. Avoid buying tortoises from pet stores or markets, as animals in these venues are often subjected to poor conditions and inadequate care. Tortoises from such sources may suffer from health problems due to improper nutrition, inadequate housing, and lack of veterinary care.

A critical consideration is whether to choose a wild-caught or captive-bred tortoise. Captive-bred tortoises are generally a better option. They tend to be healthier and are less likely to carry diseases that can be prevalent in wild populations. Additionally, wild-caught tortoises have endured the stress and trauma of being removed from their natural habitats, which can lead to long-term health issues and behavioral problems. By choosing a captive-bred tortoise, you are also supporting ethical breeding practices and reducing the demand for wild-caught animals, which can help conserve wild populations.

Ethical considerations extend beyond the source of the tortoise to the long-term commitment required to care for one. Tortoises have a remarkably long lifespan, often living for several decades. Prospective owners must be prepared for this commitment, ensuring they can provide a stable environment and consistent care for the entirety of the tortoise's life. This includes proper housing, a balanced diet, and regular veterinary check-ups. Inadequate care can lead to severe health issues and a diminished quality of life for the tortoise.

Moreover, consider the ethical implications of keeping a tortoise in captivity. These animals have specific environmental and social needs that must be met to ensure their well-being. It is important to recreate a habitat that mimics their natural environment as closely as possible, providing opportunities for the tortoise to exhibit natural behaviors.

Preparing For Arrival

Preparing for the arrival of a Russian tortoise involves careful planning and setup to ensure their health and well-being in their new home. Here's a comprehensive guide to getting everything ready before bringing your tortoise home:

First and foremost, setting up the habitat is crucial. Russian tortoises require a spacious enclosure with a secure lid to prevent escapes. The enclosure should offer enough room for the tortoise to roam comfortably and should include areas for burrowing and hiding. A suitable substrate, such as a mix of soil and sand, is ideal for burrowing behavior while avoiding substrates like pine or cedar shavings, which can be harmful.

Temperature and lighting are critical aspects of tortoise care. The enclosure should maintain a temperature gradient to allow the tortoise to regulate its body temperature effectively. A basking spot with temperatures ranging between 90-95°F (32-35°C) is essential, achieved using a heat lamp placed at one end of the enclosure. The cooler end should be maintained around 70°F (21°C). Additionally, providing UVB lighting is crucial as it helps the tortoise metabolize calcium, essential for shell and bone health.

Diet is another vital consideration. Russian tortoises are herbivores, so their diet should consist primarily of leafy greens and vegetables. Foods rich in calcium and low in protein are ideal. Avoid feeding fruits and high-protein foods, which can cause health problems in tortoises. It's essential to stock up on these appropriate foods before bringing your tortoise home.

Access to clean water is crucial for hydration and soaking. Provide a shallow dish of fresh water in the enclosure and change it daily to ensure cleanliness. Tortoises may also soak in the water dish, which helps with hydration and maintaining skin health.

Before bringing your tortoise home, ensure you have all necessary supplies ready. This includes the habitat setup, proper heating and lighting equipment, appropriate foods, and a water dish. It's also beneficial to have a designated area where the tortoise can comfortably settle into its new environment without disturbance.

Initial Health Check

When your tortoise first arrives, conducting a thorough initial health check is crucial to ensure its well-being and acclimation to its new environment. Here are the steps you should take:

Observation

Begin by carefully observing your tortoise for any signs of stress, illness, or abnormal behavior. Common indicators of health issues include lethargy, lack of appetite, unusual posture, or discharge from the eyes or nose. Stress can manifest in behaviors like hiding excessively or refusing to eat. Monitoring these signs helps in identifying potential problems early on.

Quarantine

If you already have other tortoises, it's essential to quarantine the new arrival for at least 30 days. This precautionary measure helps prevent the spread of any potential diseases or parasites to your existing tortoise population. During this period, keep the new tortoise in a separate enclosure with its own substrate, food, and water dishes. Ensure that you practice good hygiene, such as washing hands and changing clothes between handling different groups of tortoises.

Veterinary Check

Schedule a comprehensive health examination with a veterinarian who specializes in reptiles. A qualified reptile vet can conduct a thorough physical assessment, checking for overall health, any signs of illness, and specific care requirements based on the tortoise species. They will examine the tortoise's eyes, ears, nose, mouth, shell, limbs, and skin for any abnormalities or injuries.

This visit is also an opportunity to discuss dietary needs, habitat setup, and general care guidelines.

Parasite Check

During the veterinary examination, request a thorough check for both internal and external parasites. Tortoises can be susceptible to various parasites such as worms, ticks, and mites, which can compromise their health if left untreated. The vet may perform fecal tests and skin scrapings to detect parasites and recommend appropriate treatment if any are found. Prompt treatment ensures that your tortoise remains healthy and free from harmful infestations.

Hydration

Maintaining proper hydration is essential for the health of your tortoise. Tortoises may not always drink from a water dish, so offering regular soaks in shallow, lukewarm water is beneficial. These soaks not only help keep the tortoise hydrated but also assist in maintaining healthy skin and shell condition. Monitor the tortoise's response during these sessions to ensure it is comfortable and not stressed.

CHAPTER THREE

HOUSING AND ENCLOSURE

Indoor Vs. Outdoor Housing

Deciding whether to house your Russian tortoise indoors or outdoors involves careful consideration of several factors, each impacting the well-being and comfort of your pet. These factors typically include climate conditions, available space, and personal preferences regarding interaction and observation.

Indoor housing offers significant advantages in terms of creating a controlled environment. This setup helps shield the tortoise from extreme weather conditions such as excessive heat, cold, or humidity, which can be detrimental to their health. By regulating the indoor temperature and humidity levels, you can create a stable and comfortable habitat year-round. This controlled environment also minimizes the risk of exposure to predators, ensuring the safety of your tortoise at all times.

Furthermore, indoor housing allows for easier monitoring of your Russian tortoise's health and behavior. It facilitates regular observation and interaction, which can be beneficial for detecting any signs of illness or behavioral changes early on. This close supervision enables prompt intervention if needed, contributing to better overall care and well-being.

In contrast, outdoor housing offers an environment that more closely mimics the natural habitat of Russian tortoises. This setup typically provides more space for the tortoise to roam, explore, and engage in natural behaviors like burrowing and basking in natural sunlight. Outdoor enclosures can include features such as plants, rocks, and hiding spots, enriching the tortoise's environment and promoting natural behaviors.

However, outdoor housing also comes with challenges, particularly related to climate variability and predator risks. Depending on your geographical location, exposure to extreme temperatures or sudden weather changes could pose risks to your tortoise's health. Additionally, outdoor enclosures require careful predator-proofing measures to prevent access from animals that may pose a threat.

Ultimately, the decision between indoor and outdoor housing should be based on a careful assessment of these factors, tailored to the specific needs and preferences of your Russian tortoise. Some owners opt for a combination of both indoor and outdoor environments, known as a hybrid setup, to provide the benefits of both controlled conditions and naturalistic experiences.

Enclosure Setup

When preparing the ideal enclosure for your Russian tortoise, prioritizing both space and security is crucial to ensuring their well-being and happiness. Russian tortoises thrive in environments that mimic their natural habitat, providing ample room for movement and areas of security.

Begin by selecting an enclosure that is at least 4 feet long and 2 feet wide, offering sufficient space for the tortoise to roam freely. This size allows them to exhibit natural behaviors such as exploring, foraging, and basking without feeling cramped. Additionally, ensure the enclosure walls are solid and sturdy to prevent escapes and protect the tortoise from potential predators. If using a fence, make sure it is buried underground to deter digging attempts.

Creating a suitable habitat also involves providing access to both sunlight and artificial UVB lighting. Russian tortoises require UVB light to synthesize vitamin D3, which is essential for calcium metabolism and overall shell health. Place the enclosure in a location that receives natural sunlight for several hours a day, or alternatively, use UVB lamps designed for reptiles. Position the lighting fixtures at a height where the tortoise can bask within 12-18 inches to ensure they receive adequate UVB exposure.

To enhance the enclosure's functionality, consider adding various substrates and hides. Use a substrate such as a mix of topsoil, sand, and coconut fiber to mimic their natural environment and allow for digging. Provide hiding spots such as small shelters or overturned flower pots to give the tortoise places to retreat and feel secure. These features help reduce stress and encourage natural behaviors.

Maintaining proper temperature and humidity levels within the enclosure is also crucial. Russian tortoises thrive in temperatures ranging from 75°F to 85°F during the day, with a slight drop at night. Use a combination of under-tank heaters, ceramic heat emitters, or heat lamps to achieve these temperatures, ensuring there are cooler and warmer zones within the enclosure for the tortoise to regulate their body temperature as needed. Maintain a relative humidity level of around 40% to 60% by misting the enclosure daily and providing a shallow water dish for drinking and soaking.

Regularly clean and inspect the enclosure to ensure it remains a safe and hygienic environment for your Russian tortoise. Remove any uneaten food, feces, and soiled substrate promptly to prevent bacteria buildup and maintain air quality. Periodically sanitize the enclosure and accessories with a reptile-safe disinfectant to prevent the spread of diseases.

Substrate And Furnishings

Creating an ideal substrate and furnishings setup for your tortoise enclosure is crucial for mimicking its natural habitat, promoting well-being, and encouraging natural behaviors. Here's a detailed guide on selecting suitable substrate and furnishings:

Choosing the Right Substrate: The substrate you select plays a vital role in replicating your tortoise's natural environment and supporting its health. Opt for a substrate mixture that mimics the native habitat, such as a blend of soil, sand, and peat moss. This combination not only provides a natural appearance but also supports burrowing behavior, which is essential for many tortoise species. Burrowing helps them regulate body temperature and avoid extreme weather conditions.

It's crucial to avoid substrates that could potentially be ingested and cause digestive issues. Therefore, steer clear of materials like gravel, which can be accidentally consumed and lead to health complications. A fine mixture of soil and sand, enriched with peat moss for moisture retention, strikes a balance between naturalistic appearance and practical functionality.

Maintaining Humidity and Hydration: The chosen substrate should also help maintain appropriate humidity levels within the enclosure. Tortoises require certain humidity levels to thrive, depending on their species and natural habitat. The peat moss component in the substrate mixture aids in retaining moisture, creating a microenvironment that supports healthy hydration for your tortoise.

Furnishings for Enrichment: In addition to the substrate, furnishings play a crucial role in enriching your tortoise's environment. Incorporate natural elements such as rocks, logs, and plants to provide hiding spots and opportunities for climbing. These elements not only enhance the aesthetic appeal of the enclosure but also encourage natural behaviors. Tortoises often enjoy climbing over rocks and logs, which helps them stay active and engaged.

Select rocks and logs of appropriate sizes and shapes to ensure they are stable and safe for your tortoise to explore. Smooth rocks and branches without sharp edges are ideal to prevent injuries. Live or artificial plants can also be included to add greenery and stimulate natural foraging behaviors.

Maintenance and Care: Regularly monitor and maintain the substrate to ensure cleanliness and prevent mold or bacterial growth. Spot clean any soiled areas daily and replace the substrate periodically to maintain hygiene. Furnishings should also be inspected regularly for signs of wear or damage and replaced as needed to ensure your tortoise's safety.

Lighting And Temperature Requirements

Maintaining optimal lighting and temperature conditions is essential for the well-being and health of Russian tortoises (Agrionemys horsfieldii). These tortoises require specific environmental parameters to thrive in captivity, mirroring their natural habitat conditions.

Temperature Requirements:

Russian tortoises are adapted to the arid, semi-desert regions of Central Asia, where they experience significant temperature fluctuations between day and night. Replicating these conditions in captivity is crucial. During the daytime, provide a basking area equipped with a heat lamp that achieves temperatures between 95-100°F (35-38°C). This basking spot allows the tortoise to regulate its body temperature effectively, which is vital for digestion, metabolism, and overall activity levels. It's important to monitor the temperature closely using a reliable thermometer to ensure it stays within the recommended range.

Nighttime temperatures should drop to approximately 70-75°F (21-24°C). This temperature drop simulates the natural cooling that Russian tortoises experience in their native habitat during the night. Providing this nighttime cooling period is essential for their natural behavioral rhythms and overall health. Avoid significant temperature fluctuations or prolonged exposure to temperatures outside these ranges, as they can stress the tortoise and compromise its immune system.

Lighting Requirements:

In addition to temperature, adequate lighting is crucial for Russian tortoises, particularly the provision of UVB radiation. UVB light is essential for the synthesis of vitamin D3 in their skin, which is necessary for calcium metabolism. Without sufficient UVB exposure, tortoises can develop metabolic bone disease, a serious condition affecting their shell and bone health.

Use a UVB lamp specifically designed for reptiles, placing it over the basking area. Ensure the lamp provides UVB rays with an intensity and spectrum suitable for reptiles, as not all UVB bulbs are created equal. Position the lamp within the recommended distance from the basking spot, usually indicated by the manufacturer, to ensure the tortoise receives adequate UVB exposure without the risk of overexposure or burns.

Maintenance and Monitoring:

Regularly monitor both the temperature and lighting conditions within the tortoise enclosure using appropriate equipment. This includes checking temperatures daily and adjusting lamp heights or wattages as necessary to maintain the correct temperature gradients. UVB bulbs should be replaced according to the manufacturer's recommendations, as their UV output diminishes over time even if the bulb continues to emit visible light.

CHAPTER FOUR

DIET AND NUTRITION

Nutritional Needs

The Russian tortoise, a beloved reptilian pet, thrives on a carefully balanced diet essential for its overall health and well-being. Like all reptiles, these tortoises have specific nutritional requirements that must be met to ensure they remain healthy and active throughout their lives.

Fiber, a cornerstone of their diet, plays a vital role in maintaining digestive health. Russian tortoises need ample fiber to aid in proper digestion and prevent issues such as constipation. High-fiber foods like leafy greens and certain vegetables are ideal for meeting this need.

Vitamins and minerals are equally crucial for the Russian tortoise's health. These nutrients support various bodily functions, including bone health, immune function, and metabolism. Calcium, for instance, is vital for shell strength and overall skeletal integrity. A lack of essential vitamins and minerals can lead to severe health problems over time.

Protein is necessary but in moderation. Unlike some other reptiles, Russian tortoises require less protein. However, it is still essential for growth, tissue repair, and overall maintenance. They can obtain sufficient protein from sources such as dark leafy greens and occasional small amounts of insects or low-fat, high-protein plants.

A balanced diet for a Russian tortoise typically includes a variety of dark leafy greens such as dandelion greens, mustard greens, and collard greens, which provide essential vitamins and minerals. These should make up the bulk of their diet. Other vegetables like squash, bell peppers, and carrots can also be offered in moderation to add variety and additional nutrients.

Insects such as mealworms or crickets can serve as occasional treats and protein sources. It's crucial to ensure any insects offered are appropriately sized and gut-loaded (fed nutritious foods) to provide maximum nutritional benefit without overwhelming the tortoise's system with excessive protein or fat.

Water is essential for all reptiles, including Russian tortoises. They require access to fresh, clean water at all times for hydration. Tortoises may not drink water directly from a dish but may soak in shallow water regularly to maintain hydration and aid in shedding.

Supplementation may be necessary to ensure all nutritional needs are met, especially for vitamins and minerals like calcium and vitamin D3. These supplements should be carefully chosen and administered according to recommended guidelines to prevent over-supplementation, which can be harmful.

Feeding Schedule And Types Of Food

Establishing a proper feeding schedule and choosing the right types of food are crucial for maintaining the health and well-being of Russian tortoises. These herbivorous reptiles thrive on a diet primarily composed of leafy greens, supplemented with occasional treats for variety and nutritional balance.

Russian tortoises predominantly consume leafy greens as a staple. Dandelion greens, kale, and collard greens are excellent choices due to their high fiber content and essential nutrients. These greens should constitute the majority of their diet, providing essential vitamins and minerals crucial for their growth and overall health. It's important to ensure these greens are fresh and thoroughly washed to remove any pesticides or contaminants that could harm the tortoise.

In addition to leafy greens, Russian tortoises can benefit from occasional treats. These treats, such as carrots, squash, and small amounts of fruits like strawberries, offer variety and additional nutrients. However, treats should be given sparingly and in moderation to prevent dietary imbalance or obesity, which can be detrimental to their health.

A typical feeding schedule for Russian tortoises involves offering food daily. The quantity of food should be adjusted based on the tortoise's size, age, and activity level. Younger tortoises may require more frequent feedings, while adults can be fed once a day. Monitoring their weight and adjusting portion sizes accordingly helps maintain optimal health.

Fresh water should always be available for Russian tortoises, provided in a shallow dish that allows easy access. Tortoises drink water and may also soak in it to stay hydrated, especially in warmer weather or after eating dry foods.

It's essential to observe the tortoise's feeding habits and adjust the diet as needed to ensure they are receiving adequate nutrition. Over time, their dietary needs may change, requiring adjustments in the types and quantities of food offered. Consulting a veterinarian with experience in reptile care can provide guidance on specific dietary requirements and any health concerns related to nutrition.

Supplementing The Diet

Supplements are essential for maintaining the health and well-being of Russian tortoises, particularly in ensuring they receive adequate calcium and vitamin D3. These nutrients are crucial for preventing shell deformities and metabolic bone disease, common ailments in reptiles kept in captivity.

Russian tortoises, like many reptiles, require a balanced diet supplemented with calcium and vitamin D3 to support their skeletal health. In their natural habitat, they obtain these nutrients from a varied diet and exposure to sunlight. However, in captivity, replicating these conditions becomes crucial to prevent deficiencies that can lead to serious health issues.

Calcium is a fundamental mineral for the development and maintenance of a tortoise's shell and skeletal structure. Inadequate calcium intake can result in soft shells or deformities, making supplementation a vital aspect of their care routine. Calcium supplements for Russian tortoises are typically provided in powdered form, which can be dusted onto their food items. This method ensures that they ingest the necessary amount of calcium to support their growth and overall health.

Vitamin D3 is equally important as it facilitates the absorption of calcium from the digestive system. In the wild, tortoises obtain vitamin D3 through exposure to sunlight, which triggers its synthesis in the skin. However, indoor housing conditions often limit exposure to natural sunlight, necessitating dietary supplementation. Vitamin D3 supplements are carefully administered to ensure they complement the calcium intake without causing toxicity, following specific dosage guidelines tailored for reptiles.

The frequency of supplementing their diet varies based on the tortoise's age, health status, and environmental conditions. Generally, calcium and vitamin D3 supplements should be dusted onto their food several times a week. This regimen helps maintain optimal levels of these nutrients in their system, supporting bone strength and overall metabolic function.

It's crucial for tortoise owners to consult with a veterinarian or reptile specialist to determine the appropriate supplements and dosages for their specific tortoise. Factors such as diet composition, UVB lighting availability, and individual health considerations play significant roles in formulating an effective supplementation plan.

Common Dietary Issues

Russian tortoises are susceptible to various dietary issues when their nutritional requirements are not adequately met. Among these, calcium deficiency stands out as a prevalent concern, often resulting in shell softening and bone deformities. This condition underscores the importance of a calcium-rich diet and appropriate supplementation to maintain the tortoise's skeletal health.

Another critical issue is improper feeding practices, such as overfeeding or offering unsuitable foods. Feeding excessive amounts of fruits or high-protein foods can lead to obesity and digestive complications. Therefore, it is crucial to adhere to a balanced diet regimen tailored to the tortoise's specific nutritional needs. Regular monitoring of the tortoise's weight and overall health is essential to detect and address any dietary imbalances promptly.

Furthermore, some Russian tortoises may exhibit picky eating behaviors or develop specific food preferences. To mitigate these tendencies, it is beneficial to provide a diverse array of suitable foods. This approach not only ensures that the tortoise receives a spectrum of essential nutrients but also encourages healthy eating habits over time.

Effective dietary management for Russian tortoises also involves understanding their natural foraging habits and preferences. Offering foods that mimic their wild diet, such as dark leafy greens, fibrous vegetables, and occasional fruits, can contribute to their overall well-being. It is advisable to avoid foods high in oxalates, which can hinder calcium absorption, thereby exacerbating the risk of deficiencies.

In addition to dietary considerations, hydration is vital for maintaining a tortoise's health. Providing access to clean, fresh water at all times is essential, as dehydration can lead to various health issues and exacerbate existing dietary concerns.

Educating tortoise owners about proper dietary practices and regular veterinary check-ups are crucial components of responsible pet ownership. By addressing and preventing common dietary issues through informed care and observation, owners can significantly enhance the quality of life for their Russian tortoises.

CHAPTER FIVE

HEALTH AND WELLNESS

Common Health Issues

Russian tortoises, like all animals, are susceptible to a range of health issues that require attentive care to maintain their well-being. By understanding these common problems, you can effectively address and mitigate potential risks to your pet's health.

One prevalent health issue among Russian tortoises is respiratory infections. These infections often stem from environmental factors such as improper humidity levels or inadequate habitat conditions. Symptoms typically include wheezing, nasal discharge, or lethargy. Respiratory infections can escalate quickly if not promptly addressed, necessitating careful monitoring of the tortoise's habitat and immediate veterinary intervention at the first signs of illness.

Another significant concern for Russian tortoises is shell rot, a condition that develops when the shell is damaged or exposed to excessive moisture. This exposure creates a breeding ground for bacterial or fungal infections, compromising the tortoise's health. Shell rot is identifiable by discolored or soft areas on the shell, which require meticulous cleaning and treatment with antifungal or antibacterial agents under veterinary guidance. Preventive measures such as ensuring a dry, clean habitat and regular shell inspections can help mitigate the risk of shell rot.

Parasitic infestations, such as mites or worms, also pose a common threat to Russian tortoises. These parasites can significantly impact the tortoise's overall health if left untreated. Signs of parasitic infestation may include changes in behavior, weight loss, or visible signs of parasites on the tortoise's skin or in its feces. Regular veterinary check-ups and proactive parasite prevention strategies, such as maintaining cleanliness in the habitat and administering appropriate antiparasitic treatments as recommended by a veterinarian, are essential in managing and preventing parasitic infestations.

In addition to these specific health concerns, maintaining a balanced diet tailored to the nutritional needs of Russian tortoises is crucial for their overall health and immune function. A diet rich in leafy greens, vegetables, and occasional fruits, supplemented with calcium and vitamin D3, supports proper shell and bone development while enhancing their resistance to infections and diseases.

Preventative Care

Preventative care is paramount for ensuring the health and well-being of your Russian tortoise. These steps are essential to maintaining their vitality and longevity.

First and foremost, the enclosure must be meticulously maintained to provide optimal living conditions. Russian tortoises thrive in environments with specific temperature gradients and humidity levels. Aim for a basking spot around 90-95°F (32-35°C) and a cooler area around 75-85°F (24-29°C). Humidity levels should be moderate, around 50-60%, to prevent respiratory issues and shell problems. Regular monitoring with accurate thermometers and hygrometers is crucial to adjust conditions as needed.

Diet is another critical aspect of preventative care. A balanced diet is key, consisting primarily of dark, leafy greens such as kale, collard greens, and dandelion greens. These provide essential vitamins and minerals while helping to maintain proper growth and shell development. Occasional fruits like strawberries or apples can be offered as treats but should not exceed 10% of their diet to prevent digestive issues.

Maintaining a clean habitat is vital for preventing infections and other health issues. Regularly remove feces and uneaten food, and replace substrate to prevent bacterial growth. A substrate of soil, sand, or a mix thereof provides a natural environment and allows for natural behaviors like digging. Ensure hiding places are available to reduce stress, such as half logs or dense foliage, which also serve to prevent injuries by providing retreats from potential hazards.

Hydration is critical for Russian tortoises. Ensure a shallow dish of fresh, clean water is available at all times. This helps prevent dehydration and supports overall health.

Regular veterinary check-ups are essential for preventative care. A reptile-experienced veterinarian can assess overall health, provide parasite screenings, and offer advice on any specific concerns.

Recognizing Signs Of Illness

Recognizing signs of illness in your Russian tortoise is crucial for ensuring prompt treatment and maintaining their health. By observing their behavior and physical condition regularly, you can detect potential issues early, improving the chances of successful intervention and recovery.

One of the most noticeable indicators of illness in Russian tortoises is a loss of appetite. If your tortoise suddenly shows disinterest in food or eats significantly less than usual, it could be a sign of underlying health problems. Alongside this, changes in fecal patterns—such as diarrhea or unusual consistency—should also be noted. Healthy tortoise feces are typically firm and well-formed, so any deviations should be investigated.

Lethargy is another common symptom of illness. If your tortoise appears unusually sluggish or spends more time than usual resting and not engaging in normal activities, it may indicate an underlying health issue. This lethargy can be accompanied by behavioral changes, such as increased hiding or aggression, which are often responses to discomfort or pain.

Respiratory issues are particularly concerning and may manifest as audible wheezing or difficulty breathing. Tortoises with respiratory problems may exhibit open-mouth breathing or noticeable efforts to breathe, which require immediate veterinary attention to prevent further complications.

Regularly inspecting your tortoise's shell is essential. Any abnormalities such as soft spots, discoloration, or signs of shell rot—characterized by foul odor or visible deterioration—should be addressed promptly. Shell health reflects overall well-being in tortoises, so changes in its appearance can indicate systemic health issues.

In addition to physical symptoms, monitoring for changes in behavior is critical. Tortoises normally have predictable routines, so any sudden shifts, such as increased aggression or withdrawal, could signal distress or illness. These changes often prompt further investigation, including veterinary assessment to identify and address the underlying cause.

Regular veterinary care is crucial for ensuring the health and well-being of your Russian tortoise. These reptiles require specialized attention from a veterinarian experienced in reptile care to address their unique needs effectively. Scheduled check-ups play a pivotal role in maintaining their health, offering opportunities for comprehensive examinations and personalized guidance on diet, habitat conditions, and overall husbandry practices.

During routine veterinary visits, a reptile-experienced veterinarian conducts thorough examinations to assess your Russian tortoise's physical condition. This includes checking for signs of illness, monitoring weight and growth patterns, and examining the eyes, mouth, skin, and shell for any abnormalities. Such examinations are instrumental in early detection of health issues, allowing timely intervention to prevent complications.

Diagnostic tests are also integral to the veterinary care regimen for Russian tortoises. These may include fecal exams to detect internal parasites, which are common in reptiles and can significantly impact their health if left untreated. Additionally, blood work may be performed to evaluate organ function and detect metabolic imbalances or infectious diseases. These tests provide critical insights into your tortoise's internal health, guiding the veterinarian in tailoring specific treatment or dietary adjustments as necessary.

In cases of illness or injury, prompt veterinary attention is paramount. Russian tortoises, like all reptiles, may conceal signs of illness until they are quite advanced. Therefore, any observed changes in behavior, appetite, or activity levels should prompt immediate consultation with a veterinarian. Early intervention not only enhances treatment success but also minimizes stress and discomfort for the tortoise.

Beyond reactive care, veterinarians also offer proactive advice on preventive measures. This includes recommendations for creating an optimal habitat environment, ensuring proper temperatures and humidity levels, and advising on suitable substrate and furnishings. Such guidance helps mitigate the risk of health problems associated with inadequate husbandry practices.

Educating yourself about your Russian tortoise's specific needs and behaviors is also crucial. A knowledgeable veterinarian can provide educational resources on topics such as handling techniques, dietary requirements, and recognizing behavioral cues indicative of stress or illness. This empowers you to provide attentive care and promptly address any emerging issues in collaboration with your veterinary team.

CHAPTER SIX

BEHAVIOR AND SOCIALIZATION

Understanding Russian Tortoise Behavior

Russian tortoises are beloved for their serene and gentle nature. Their behavior is predominantly diurnal, meaning they are most active during the day. Much of their daily routine revolves around essential activities like foraging for food and basking in sunlight, crucial for maintaining their health and regulating body temperature.

In their natural habitat, Russian tortoises exhibit instinctual behaviors such as burrowing to escape extreme temperatures and seeking shelter for safety. These behaviors are also observable in captive environments, where they often establish distinct territories within their enclosures. Owners can deepen their understanding of these tortoises by observing how they interact with their surroundings, reflecting their innate tendencies despite being in captivity.

Solitary by nature, Russian tortoises typically prefer to roam and feed alone, mirroring their behavior in the wild even when kept as pets. Each tortoise may display unique preferences and habits influenced by factors like age, health status, and environmental conditions. By attentively observing their pet tortoises, owners can glean valuable insights into their personalities and needs.

Maintaining a conducive environment is crucial for ensuring the well-being of Russian tortoises. Providing ample space for exploration and adequate access to basking spots is essential. This setup not only supports their natural behaviors but also promotes their overall health and longevity. Additionally, offering a varied diet rich in leafy greens and occasional fruits ensures nutritional balance, contributing to their vitality.

Interaction with humans may vary among individual tortoises; some may show curiosity while others may prefer minimal handling. Respecting their preferences fosters trust and reduces stress, enhancing their quality of life.

Regular health checks by a veterinarian familiar with reptiles are recommended to monitor their physical condition and address any emerging issues promptly.

Handling And Interaction

Handling a Russian tortoise requires a gentle and considerate approach due to their sensitivity to sudden movements and loud noises. These reptiles, known for their calm demeanor and small size compared to other tortoise species, benefit from interactions that prioritize their comfort and well-being.

When engaging with a Russian tortoise, it's essential to allow them to initiate contact whenever possible. This approach respects their natural instincts and helps build trust over time. Sudden movements or loud noises can startle them, leading to stress responses that may negatively impact their health. Therefore, a calm and patient demeanor from the handler is crucial.

Proper handling techniques involve supporting the tortoise's body correctly to prevent any potential injury. Russian tortoises should be gently lifted, ensuring that their weight is evenly distributed and supported, especially around their limbs and shell. This method not only protects the tortoise from harm but also promotes a sense of security during human interaction.

Regular, gentle handling sessions can acclimate Russian tortoises to human presence and reduce fear responses.

Consistency in handling helps them become accustomed to being touched and held, fostering a positive association with human interaction. Over time, this familiarity can contribute to a more relaxed demeanor and less stress during handling sessions.

It's important to recognize that individual tortoises may vary in their tolerance for handling. While some may enjoy and benefit from regular interaction, others may prefer minimal handling and more observational care. Understanding and respecting these preferences is crucial for their well-being and overall comfort.

Observing the tortoise's body language during handling can provide valuable cues about their comfort level. Signs of stress, such as withdrawing into their shell, hissing, or attempting to escape, indicate that the tortoise may need a break or prefers less interaction at that moment. Respecting these signals helps maintain a positive and trusting relationship between the tortoise and its handler.

Enrichment Activities

Enrichment activities play a pivotal role in maintaining the health and well-being of Russian tortoises, encompassing both mental stimulation and physical exercise. These activities are essential as they mimic the natural behaviors and environments that tortoises would experience in the wild.

A fundamental aspect of enriching a Russian tortoise's enclosure involves providing a diverse range of textures and surfaces. This can include incorporating rocks of varying sizes, logs, and live plants. These elements not only diversify the tortoise's environment but also encourage exploration and natural behaviors such as climbing over rocks or navigating around plants. By simulating different textures, the tortoise engages its senses and maintains physical dexterity, crucial for overall health.

Introducing safe toys and objects further enhances enrichment. Items such as hollowed logs or specially designed tortoise toys that encourage digging or burrowing activities are beneficial. These activities mimic behaviors seen in their natural habitat, promoting physical activity and preventing boredom. Toys can also serve as focal points for mental engagement, as tortoises investigate and interact with them, stimulating their curiosity and cognitive abilities.

Feeding time presents another opportunity for enrichment. Russian tortoises thrive on a varied diet consisting primarily of leafy greens and vegetables, supplemented occasionally with fruits. Offering a wide array of food items not only ensures nutritional balance but also taps into their instinctual foraging behaviors. Scatter feeding, where food is spread across the enclosure, encourages the tortoise to actively search for and consume different food items, much like they would in the wild. This promotes natural feeding behaviors and keeps the tortoise mentally engaged during meal times.

It is crucial for owners to be mindful of food safety and suitability. All food items should be thoroughly researched to ensure they are safe for tortoises to consume, free from pesticides or harmful additives. Freshness and variety are key to providing a nutritionally rich diet that supports the tortoise's overall health and vitality.

Socialization With Other Tortoises

Socializing Russian tortoises, although they are solitary creatures in their natural habitats, can be managed effectively with careful planning and monitoring. Introducing tortoises to each other requires meticulous oversight to prevent aggression and ensure minimal stress. Providing sufficient space and resources for each tortoise is crucial to allow them to establish territories and reduce competition.

In the wild, Russian tortoises typically live alone, but in captivity, they can coexist peacefully under certain conditions. Socialization among these tortoises can offer various benefits, such as opportunities for natural behaviors like mating rituals and occasional social interaction. However, it's essential to recognize that not all tortoises will thrive in social settings. Individual personalities and preferences play a significant role in determining whether a tortoise will enjoy social company or prefer solitude.

When introducing Russian tortoises to each other, careful observation is paramount. Monitoring their interactions closely allows for early intervention if aggression arises, which helps prevent injuries and reduces stress. Each tortoise should have access to its own hideaways, basking spots, and food to minimize competition and ensure they feel secure in their environment.

Creating a conducive environment for socialization involves providing ample space where tortoises can retreat if they feel overwhelmed or threatened. This setup mimics their natural habitats, where they have the freedom to roam and establish their territories without feeling overcrowded or insecure. Natural substrates and vegetation can also enhance their living conditions, promoting a sense of familiarity and comfort.

Furthermore, understanding the signs of stress or discomfort in Russian tortoises is crucial during socialization attempts. These signs may include decreased appetite, hiding behavior, or aggression. Adjustments to the environment or separating tortoises may be necessary if these signs persist, ensuring the well-being of each individual.

CHAPTER SEVEN

BREEDING AND REPRODUCTION

Mating Behavior

Russian tortoises, much like many reptiles, display distinct mating behaviors that are heavily influenced by seasonal changes and environmental cues. Typically, the mating season for Russian tortoises aligns with the arrival of spring and early summer, a time when temperatures begin to rise, signaling the onset of heightened reproductive activity. During this period, male tortoises exhibit increased activity levels, driven by innate instincts to seek out potential mates.

Male Russian tortoises engage in elaborate courtship rituals to attract females. This includes behaviors such as chasing and nudging females, often using their front legs to assert dominance or to displace rival males. Competition among males can be fierce during this time, with individuals occasionally attempting to flip over their rivals to secure mating opportunities.

Conversely, female Russian tortoises undergo physiological changes that make them receptive to mating advances during the breeding season. They may display signs of interest by allowing males to approach and mount them, indicating readiness for copulation. Once a pair has formed, copulation itself is a carefully orchestrated event, often lasting several minutes to ensure successful fertilization. This process is crucial for the female tortoise, as it marks the beginning of egg development and eventual nesting.

The mating behavior of Russian tortoises is intricately tied to hormonal shifts triggered by seasonal transitions. As temperatures rise and daylight hours increase, these reptiles experience a surge in reproductive hormones, prompting them to engage in behaviors necessary for mating and reproduction. While instinct plays a significant role in guiding these behaviors, environmental factors such as temperature and humidity also play crucial roles in signaling the optimal conditions for mating and subsequent nesting.

After mating, female Russian tortoises undergo a process of preparing for egg laying, a pivotal phase in their reproductive cycle. They actively seek out suitable nesting sites characterized by loose, well-drained soil, typically favoring sunny locations. Once a suitable spot is found, they meticulously dig shallow nests, a behavior that reflects their instinctive care for ensuring optimal conditions for their offspring.

Within these carefully excavated nests, female Russian tortoises deposit their clutch of eggs, usually numbering between 2 to 5 eggs. The exact number can vary based on the individual tortoise's size and overall health. Each egg is delicately buried by the female, a protective measure aimed at shielding them from potential predators and providing an environment conducive to successful incubation.

Incubation of Russian tortoise eggs is a critical stage that significantly influences the development and eventual hatching of the offspring. The ambient temperature within the nesting site plays a pivotal role in this process, as it directly impacts the sex determination of the hatchlings. Warmer temperatures generally tend to produce more female tortoises, while cooler temperatures typically result in more males. This natural mechanism underscores the species' adaptation to environmental conditions, ensuring a balanced population over time.

The incubation period for Russian tortoise eggs typically spans from 60 to 90 days under natural conditions. Throughout this duration, the buried eggs remain undisturbed, benefiting from the stable environment provided by the soil. This period is crucial for the embryos to develop fully, drawing upon the nutrients stored within the eggs during their formation.

During incubation, the female tortoise may exhibit periodic visits to the nesting site, though her direct involvement in the process diminishes once the eggs are laid and buried. This behavior aligns with their instinctual understanding of maternal care, ensuring minimal disturbance to the developing eggs while they progress towards hatching.

Overall, the egg laying and incubation process in Russian tortoises exemplifies their adaptive reproductive strategies honed through evolution. From the meticulous selection of nesting sites to the careful burial of eggs and the crucial role of temperature in sex determination, each step underscores their resilience and adaptability in natural environments. This reproductive cycle not only perpetuates the species but also highlights the intricate balance between environmental factors and biological imperatives in the natural world.

Once the incubation period concludes, hatchlings emerge from their eggs, beginning their journey into the world. Russian tortoise hatchlings exhibit impressive independence from the outset, instinctively digging their way out of nests to embark on quests for sustenance and shelter. These miniature replicas of adults possess an immediate need for a suitable habitat, one that provides warmth, shelter, and ample vegetation.

Critical to hatchling care is ensuring they receive a diet rich in vegetation, essential for their growth and development. Leafy greens such as dandelion greens, collard greens, and turnip greens are excellent choices, providing necessary vitamins and minerals. Supplementing their diet with calcium is vital for healthy shell development, typically provided through powdered calcium sprinkled on their food.

Creating an optimal environment for hatchlings is crucial for their well-being. A warm enclosure, mimicking their natural habitat, helps them adjust and thrive. This can be achieved with a combination of a heat lamp or heating pad set to maintain temperatures around 85-90°F (29-32°C) during the day, with a slight drop at night to around 75-80°F (24-27°C). This temperature gradient allows hatchlings to regulate their body temperature effectively.

The enclosure should also offer security, minimizing stress and providing hiding spots. A substrate of soil mixed with sand replicates their natural environment and supports their digging behavior. Hatchlings, like their adult counterparts, enjoy burrowing, which aids thermoregulation and provides a sense of security.

Regular monitoring of their behavior and health is essential. Hatchlings should be active and curious, exploring their surroundings. Any signs of lethargy, loss of appetite, or abnormal behavior should prompt immediate attention to prevent health complications.

Hydration is another critical aspect of hatchling care. While they derive some moisture from their diet, providing a shallow dish of fresh water ensures they remain adequately hydrated. Ensure the water is changed regularly to prevent contamination.

As hatchlings grow, their dietary and environmental needs will evolve. Gradually introduce new foods and adjust the enclosure as they develop. Regular veterinary check-ups are recommended to monitor growth and address any health concerns promptly.

Challenges In Breeding Russian Tortoises

Breeding Russian tortoises can be a highly rewarding endeavor, but it also presents several challenges that breeders must navigate carefully to ensure successful outcomes. One of the primary challenges involves creating and maintaining suitable environmental conditions for both mating and egg incubation. In captivity, replicating the natural habitat of Russian tortoises is crucial. This includes meticulously controlling factors such as temperature gradients and lighting cycles, which are pivotal in triggering reproductive behaviors and supporting the healthy development of eggs.

A significant concern in breeding Russian tortoises is the preservation of genetic diversity and the avoidance of inbreeding. Inbreeding can result in genetic weaknesses and health issues among offspring, underscoring the importance of selecting breeding pairs with diverse genetic backgrounds. Breeders often conduct thorough genetic assessments to minimize these risks and ensure the long-term health and vitality of the population.

Managing hatchlings is another critical aspect of breeding Russian tortoises. Newly hatched tortoises are particularly vulnerable to predators, diseases, and environmental stressors. Providing meticulous care from the moment of hatching is essential to their survival and development. This includes offering a balanced diet rich in calcium and other essential nutrients to support healthy growth and shell development.

Furthermore, monitoring the growth and development of hatchlings is essential. Breeders track each tortoise's progress closely to detect any signs of health issues early on. This proactive approach allows for timely intervention and ensures that hatchlings reach maturity under optimal conditions.

Successful breeding programs also involve ongoing education and collaboration among breeders to share knowledge and best practices. This helps in addressing emerging challenges and refining breeding techniques over time. Additionally, engaging with veterinary experts can provide invaluable support in managing the health and welfare of both adult tortoises and their offspring.

☐

THE END